Bus (603) 436-4310
Fax (603) 436-4937

TIMOTHY J. "TED" CONNORS
Chairman
New Hampshire Pari-Mutuel Commission

P.O. Box 92
Portsmouth, NH 03801

PORTSMOUTH &
Coastal New Hampshire

A PHOTOGRAPHIC PORTRAIT

TWIN LIGHTS PUBLISHERS

Other Titles by
TWIN LIGHTS PUBLISHERS

Greater Newburyport: A Photographic Portrait

Other Titles by
PILOTPRESS & TWIN LIGHTS PUBLISHERS

Cape Ann: A Photographic Portrait

Kittery to the Kennebunks: A Photographic Portrait

*The Mystic Coast–Stonington to New London:
A Photographic Portrait*

Boston's South Shore: A Photographic Portrait

The White Mountains: A Photographic Portrait

Upper Cape Cod: A Photographic Portrait

The Rhode Island Coast: A Photographic Portrait

First published in the United States of America by
Twin Lights Publishers, Inc.
Ten Hale Street
Rockport, Massachusetts 01966
Telephone: (978) 546-7398

ISBN 1-885435-13-4

10 9 8 7 6 5 4 3 2

Printed in China

Designer: Leeann Leftwich

Cover image:
Chris Fitt
Whaleback Light
At the entrance to one of the nation's earliest
settlements, Whaleback Light stands sentinel. Once
a world-class trade center, then a gritty seaport,
Portsmouth Harbor has evolved into the ideal mix
of history, mystery, culture and commerce. If you
lived here, you'd be home.

PORTSMOUTH &
Coastal New Hampshire

A PHOTOGRAPHIC PORTRAIT

TWIN LIGHTS PUBLISHERS

TABLE OF CONTENTS

Tammy Byron
Staying Power

Few local mariners today know the ghostly tale of Jack
Ringbolt. Born aboard a sailing ship, Jack died in
Portsmouth. Friends buried him at the mouth of the
Piscataqua, weighed down by canon shot. Legend says
Jack arose in flames, spirited away, and was spotted by
a Portsmouth clipper one thousand miles from home.

INTRODUCTION

While we are thanking the people who made this book possible, we should not forget Captain John Smith, who visited our Seacoast in 1614. Smith convinced his English supporters that "Northern Virginia"—as he called it—was a great place to settle. He especially liked the Isles of Shoals near a fast flowing river the natives called "Pascataway." We should thank David and his wife Amais Thompson, the Granite State's first settlers, who arrived at Odiorne's Point in Rye in 1623. And let's not forget King George who gave New Hampshire its own royal governor, separate from the Puritan colonies of Massachusetts and Maine on either side. It was that decision more than any, perhaps, that made this tiny coastline unique.

Others have visited and spread the word about the special charm of Portsmouth. That list includes George Washington, Lafayette, Paul Revere, John Paul Jones, Daniel Webster. Writers from Celia Thaxter and John Greenleaf Whittier to Anita Shreve have been captivated as well.

It is the artists after all, painters and poets, and the photographers in this book, who continually remind us how precious this tiny strip of coastline really is. Through this book they have given us, not only a record of how the Portsmouth area appears today—but a vision of how we want it to remain.

You now hold that vision in your hands. Sprinkled among the pictures, you can read a bit of local history, legend and lore. Whether you live in Seacoast, New Hampshire or simply visit, you can share in the preservation of its resources and its history. For helping keep our region as beautiful and vital as ever—we thank you too.

FIRST PRIZE

Kelvin Edwards
Fogged Fort

Best known for light house, Fort Point Light is also called Fort Constitution, Fort William & Mary and Newcastle Light. Other early fortifications in the area include Fort Dearborn in Rye, Fort Foster and Fort McClary in Kittery, Fort Stark, also in New Castle and the former Fort Star on the Isles of Shoals.

Originally from Alabama, Kevin Edwards is a retired engineer from the Portsmouth Naval Shipyard. Photography has been his avocation for more than 20 years. Kevin searches, he says, only for images that he finds pleasing and is driven by no commercial goals. A resident of Kittery, Maine now for 34 years, he tends toward scenic shots. His winning picture was taken one day in June while on New Castle Common. The fog rolled in and he turned to capture a haunting image of the lighthouse nearby.

SECOND PRIZE

Chris Fitt

River Dream

The tugs arise at dawn to guide the great ships in.
As the tankers glide near shore they move like
silent villages. But deep in the cold water, as the
great propellers churn, those who sleep along the
river banks can feel the boats arrive—and roll
silently in their dreams.

*Chris Fitt describes himself as a "semi-professional"
photographer on his way toward a full time career.
He currently works in a Portsmouth camera shop
and shoots weddings and portraits as well. Among
his part time jobs was a summer of work on the
tall ship HMS Bounty. Born to the Seacoast, NH
area, Chris studied photojournalism in Miami. He
lives right in downtown Portsmouth, NH with his
wife Deborah and their two children.*

THIRD PRIZE

Harry Lichtman

A New World

European interest in the mysterious "new world" inspired more than Columbus and the Pilgrims. An explorer in the first decade of the 1600s reported seeing as many as 200 ships along the shores of New England. A few followed dreams of gold, but like NH founders David and Amais Thompson, expected to work hard.

For Harry Lichtman, photography is a natural extension of his love for outdoor sports like hiking, backpacking and kayaking. Although he has had no formal training, Harry is a member of the New Hampshire Society of Photographic Artists. His work has recently been seen at the League of NH Craftsmen and in publications by the Appalachian Mountain Club and Eastern Mountain Sports. He lives in Newmarket, NH.

Daniel Caldwell
Sagamore Creek

Barely two miles from the city
center, a winter kayak put in
here will be drawn toward the
rambling waterfront mid-1700s
mansion of NH's royal British
governor, now open to the
public. Veer right and the river
brings the visitor up behind the
Wentworth-by-the-Sea hotel.

PORTSMOUTH &
THE ISLES OF SHOALS

Jeremy Burnham
South End

This picturesque view of
Portsmouth's residential South
End presents a waterfront not
unlike it might have appeared
150 years ago. In its time the
area has been home to wealthy
British landholders and to
ethnic immigrant families.
Today walking the narrow
streets, one can almost touch the
houses on both sides at once.

Christy Labrie
White Light

In the 1840s Thomas Laighton
moved his family from downtown Portsmouth to White
Island light. His daughter, writer
Celia Thaxter, was just four
when she arrived for a ten year
stay. Her 1873 book "Among
the Isles of Shoals" remains the
most captivating guide to the
Isles yet written

Marc Edwards

City Lights

For a city of only 26,000, Portsmouth puts on the dog at night. Visitors find a half dozen theaters, ballet, street performers and more restaurants per capita than any city around. The transition from hard-scrabble sailor's port to cultural capital is complete.

Rockport Publishers
Portsmouth Harbor

Seen from the air, Portsmouth
Harbor is more water than
earth. A network of intercon-
nected islands and inlets come
together at New Castle, Kittery
and Portsmouth. Left alone in
a dory, many residents would
find it a tricky task to navigate
a watery route home.

R I G H T

Rockport Publishers
Nine Rocky Isles

While almost no one lives year
round on the privately owned
Isles of Shoals today, in the
colonial era the islands teamed
with hundreds of fishermen.
Duck, Appledore, Malaga,
Smuttynose and Cedar are in
Maine while Star, Lunging,
Seaveys and White islands are
in NH.

Christy Labrie
Mary Caswell's Memorial

On Star Island, ten miles to sea Mary has found peace under the watchful eye of White Island Light. Several graves of early settlers stand silently to remind us of the early history of the fishing outposts on the Isles of Shoals. Even today some fishermen use the area for lobstering and draggers will seek protection in Gosport Harbor when the sea kicks up.

OPPOSITE

Reid Bunker
Ten Miles Out

Just below the stony Gosport Chapel on rugged Star Island visitors are surprised to find a distant museum. The Vaughan Cottage is both a quiet restful reading room and a fascinating small library dedicated to the poet Celia Thaxter and her brother Oscar Laighton who lived all his 99 years here.

TOP

Andrew Douglass
Tugboat Alley

Ceres Street still retains a wisp of its hard-knuckle maritime heritage. When Portsmouth was a rowdy seaport, these were grain warehouses. A Hollywood interpretation of this street can be seen at the opening of the 1940 film "Northwest Passage" starring the unlikely Walter Brennan and Robert Young as Portsmouth natives.

ABOVE

Mary Johanna Brown
Square Café

All roads lead to Market Square, which has become a year-round gathering place for visitors and "townies" of all ages. As early as March, thanks to global warming, diners take to the outdoor cafes. Widened to accommodate pedestrians, the renovated sidewalks and square still function as a New England common—minus the farm animals.

ABOVE

Harry Lichtman
Separate Peace

Perfectly peaceful, it's no
wonder that Sagamore Creek became home in the
19th century to a well known local hermit. Who
could blame him? Canoeists and kayakers today
seek the same solace along its briny waters.

LEFT

Mary Johanna Brown
City Forrest

Tucked neatly away in a copse of trees on the edge
of town, the Urban Forestry Center is a surprise
even to many residents. Other surprise tour sites
include the Wentworth-Gardner and Wentworth-
Coolidge mansions on the river, both stunning 18th
century mansions, sites well worth seeking out.

OPPOSITE

Backstage Army

Thanks to the volunteer militia of Pro Portsmouth,
the annual Market Square Day goes off like clock-
work. Hours before the festival—stages appear,
booths sprout up, balloon arches rise—to greet up to
200,000 visitors. By dawn the day after, the downtown is so perfectly clean, it all seems like a dream.
Photo courtesy of Pro Portsmouth

Andrew Douglass
Harbor Lights

Already an established shipbuilding center in the late 1600s, Portsmouth holds tenaciously to its role as an active industrial port. In the 1700s this small natural harbor was bounded on both sides by the Massachusetts Bay Colony, while New Hampshire's only port was ruled by an independent – and very wealthy – British governor.

ABOVE

Jeremy Burnham
A Good Day for the Fish

Fog-bound fishing boats cluster at the city's small but thriving commercial fishing pier off Pierce Island. As early as the 1500s, dried and salted "dunned" fish from this region was a staple food in Europe though it had to be soaked in water and beaten with a hammer before eating.

RIGHT

Judith A. Graham
River View

Visitors who travel the region only by highway miss the best of the Seacoast. It is meant to be seen by boat. These are the original roads where docks replace garages and small boats supplant cars. Only from this perspective can one know the Piscataqua.

OPPOSITE

Edgar W. Ohman
Passing Centuries

HMS Bounty, used in the Marlon Brando film "Mutiny on the Bounty," glides into Portsmouth Harbor. This replica of an 18th century vessel, passing the 19th century lighthouse, was the last 20th century visit by a tall ship to Portsmouth.

ABOVE

Eric H. O'Brien
Yard Sail

One of the first photographs in the US Navy archives shows Old Ironsides being refit here at the Portsmouth Naval Shipyard. Built on a series of islands on the Kittery side of the river, the "Yard" has been a source of local jobs and pride for 200 years.

Douglas Bolko

Worlds Apart

Separated by only a few
hundred feet of river, Kittery and
Portsmouth can seem worlds
away. In the colonial area, forts
on the Maine side were built for
protection against seizure of Maine
goods by NH taxmen. The towns
still share their common heritage
like two rambunctious brothers.

Kelvin Edwards

Uplifting Story

Road traffic between Kittery and
Portsmouth finally began in 1923
when a five year old girl named
Eileen Dondero cut the ribbon to
open the Memorial Bridge.
Recently automated, the historic
span bridge was rededicated in
1998 by Eileen Dondero Foley
herself. Still politically active, the
little girl had grown up to become
mayor of Portsmouth.

ABOVE

Andrew Douglass
Piscataqua Tugs

Like the lowly gundalows before them, the tugboats of Portsmouth have been critical to the life of the port city. A local author has written an entire book chronicling every Piscataqua tug, including the Nancy Moran in the foreground built in 1958.

OPPOSITE

Andrew Douglass
Iron Workhorses

Portsmouth's famous tugs are not for show, but truly hardworking vessels. The deep Piscataqua River owns one of the world's fastest and challenging tides, and these tugs are required to smooth the way for everything from oil tankers and atomic subs to tall ships.

TOP

Matthew Hadfield
King's Woods

Once Portsmouth was a dense forest so spectacular that British settlers established a logging industry here. Used for masts and ships, trees more than two feet in diameter were the official property of the king, and the most powerful role in colonial New Hampshire was to be surveyor of the king's woods.

ABOVE

Gregory E. Smart
Gosport View

From the tip of Star Island at the Isles of Shoals, looking back toward the former Gosport Village, the Rev. Tuck Monument points skyward. In Tuck's time, this area was barren rock. Beloved of the hard-drinking "heathen" fishermen, Tuck was paid in valuable "quintals of fish." He became one of wealthiest clerics in the colonies.

ABOVE
Andrew Douglass

Sarah Long

Ferry service remained the primary means of crossing the Piscatqua to Kittery, Maine until the early 20th century. The Sarah Mildred Long Bridge, named for a longtime port employee, was the site of a toll bridge and railroad crossing. At its base deep in the river, is the wreck of a railroad train still visited by local divers.

NEXT PAGE, LEFT
Marianne P. Young

Timelessness

There is a moment, people around here know well, when all time stops. Perhaps the world continues elsewhere, but on the Piscataqua nothing moves, save the slapping of waves against a darkened boat or a gliding bird silhouetted against a blazing sky.

NEXT PAGE, RIGHT
Marianne P. Young

River Wisdom

The NH seacoast may be small, but there are many miles to travel inland along the Lamprey, Cochecho, Oyster, Exeter and Bellamy rivers. Here the first few plantations were granted by royal decree, forming the key towns of the Piscataqua River, sometimes called the drowned river valley.

Jeremy Burnham
Ebb Tide

Living in New England by the sea, it is impossible to ignore the rhythms of Nature. A lone skiff evidences the daily cycle of seawater to mud that leaves inexperienced navigators at the mercy of the tide. Knowing when to wait and when to row is the river's first lesson.

Terry Chick
Down South

The revitalized South End has become the trendy place to live in Portsmouth. Firm guidelines from the Historic District Commission preserve the look and feel of the area once populated by early settlers and immigrant families. Others voice concern over the need for alternative affordable housing to support the diverse population that gives the city its unique energy.

Terry Chick
Old Strawbery Banke

The serene Strawbery Banke Museum area was once the thriving neighborhood of Puddledock. The actual 1630s settlement by that name was located a short distance upriver. The name "Portsmouth" was not applied to the region officially until the 1650s. Before that Native Americans called it "Piscataway".

Terry Chick
Recycled Brick

Now an office on Daniel Street, this building was the City Hall (now in the former hospital) and before that the local high school. It has been noted that the city's unchanging character is due, in part, to the Yankee maxim: "Waste not, want not."

D. Anne Murphy
Save Our Station

A new sunrise, perhaps, for the Search and Rescue Station visible in the distance on Wood Island. Preservationists are working to save the historic site where brave men once hurtled boats down a wooden ramp and plunged into deadly frigid water to rescue troubled mariners.

LEFT

Stephen Gianotti
Back Channel

In 1905 the largest dynamite explosion in the world at that time changed the shape of the Piscataqua. Henderson's Point blew up and traffic flow moved to the wider part of the river. But boaters can still take the lazy back channel around the Navy Yard where a small marina hides.

Teresa L. Fitzpatrick

You Will Come Back

For 125 years patrons of the Oceanic Hotel on Star Island have found themselves compelled to return to the sparsely beautiful Isles of Shoals. Privately owned, the hotel offers summer conferees communal dining, Spartan living, two showers a week and the most glorious sunsets on Earth.

R I G H T

Louise Y. Barsalou

Solid Appeal

Portsmouth's strong visual image so popular with photographers and artists comes from a blend of industrial-strength architecture and more delicate colonial features. This downtown doorway manages to be attractive, yet distant.

Lone Boat

Marianne P. Young

This is a world of fiberglass, rayon, aluminum and high speed "personalized watercraft". All of them put together cannot match the beauty and strength of a single wooden rowboat. This hand-made whery is the epitome of Yankee design and construction—poetry that floats.

Marianne P. Young
Mill Pond Swan

In Durham the swans of naturalists Lorne and Margaret Milne are well known. Their study of a family of wild birds attracted national interest and now the feathered descendants of the original pair populate both legend and rivers.

Marianne P. Young
Fresh Angle

You see them all about, men and women and children with long thin poles and miles of twine dipped in the water. They hang on bridges, breakwaters, boats and beaches. They seem intent on something far away—but what they can all be doing remains unclear.

ABOVE

Marianne P. Young

Night Riders

Traffic through Portsmouth, it appears, is not going to slow down. Equidistant from Manchester, Concord, the NH Lakes, Portland, ME and Boston, MA, the city is highly accessible by car. Now there is airline service to Pease Tradeport, visiting cruise ships and the planned return of passenger trains.

LEFT

Andrew Douglass

Market Square

Leading out of Market Square, this street was originally called King Street. The name seemed inappropriate after the Revolution and was quickly changed to Congress Street for President George Washington's visit in 1789. Today the modernized square is known for its architecture, shops and enormous variety of restaurants.

BELOW

Terry Chick

Back to Sea

Having offloaded upriver, tankers catch the full tide back below the Interstate and two lift bridges toward the other side of the world. In the 19th century famous Piscataqua clippers made similar runs under sail to distant nations and for generations the harbor was as filled with fluttering cloth, one author writes, as the clothes lines of an orphanage.

Andrew Douglass

Cold Steeple

Market Square in winter would be familiar to a time traveling visitor from the 1850s. The only surprise would be the white North Church steeple which, in bygone days, was painted a milk chocolate brown. The area was formerly known as The Parade.

Andrew Douglass

Still Inspiring

According to the plaque on the Old North Church, this is where George Washington and Daniel Webster worshipped while in town. In fact, they attended services on this very spot in an earlier wooden church. In their day the Old State House stood right in front of the church.

Jeremy Burnham

Snow Time

New Englanders measure their lives against the weather. Hail storms and hurricanes are woven into family histories like relatives. This recent Middle Street snowfall is a reminder of the storm of 1886 when trees and telegraph wires collapsed and snow on the street was tamped flat by teams of oxen dragging heavy logs.

Andrew Douglas

Blazing Yule

Three historic fires in the early 1800s destroyed hundreds of wooden buildings in what is now Market Square. Everything from here to the river was devastated and builders were required, by law, to replace structures only with the brick buildings visible today. Ironically all three fires took place on Christmas week.

Andrew Douglass
Red Flowers, Red Lights

Hard to believe that a century ago this was the heart of Portsmouth's "red light" district where more than a dozen houses of ill repute plied their trade. Once called Water Street, the area was purchased and sanitized by the plucky Prescott sisters for whom the park here is named.

Sherry L. Raymond
Looking Back

Thousands of visitors to the park never notice. Bustling by with their digital cameras, backpacks and water bottles, they miss the subtle truth. But as this amazing photo clearly shows, the flowers of Prescott Park have begun to jostle for a good look back at the tourists.

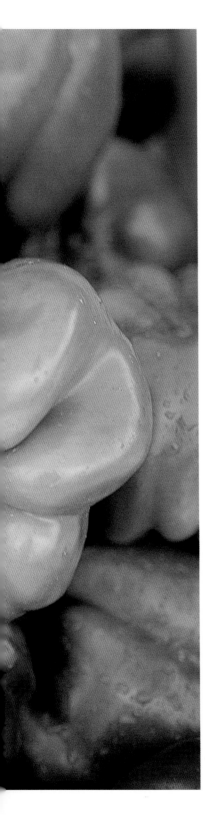

Marianne P. Young
Farmer's Market

Through the cooperation of local growers, the concept of a weekly farm marketplace has returned to the Seacoast. Residents and visitors now make a bee-line once each week for the outdoor stands, reviving an age old tradition of local consumption of local goods.

Marianne P. Young
Shared Bounty

One rarely known NH fact involves a visit by Myles Standish to David Thompson of Rye in 1623. Starving Plymouth colonists needed food, he said, so Thompson brought salted-cod to his only Euro-New England neighbors. The result according to a Pilgrim diary, was the second colonial day of "thanksgiving" —courtesy of Seacoast NH.

Marianne P. Young
Purple Reign

The earliest colonists in Portsmouth's Strawbery Banke experiment were wholly dependent on their English financiers for food and supplies. It looked, for awhile, as if the New England area would not support the crops needed for survival.

L E F T

Marianne P. Young
North Plantation

Recent research for the Portsmouth Black History Trail has proven that slave labor was not just, as many Yankees believe, "a southern problem." The wealthy Langdon family, for example, enslaved African workers to manage their Portsmouth family farm long before the Revolution.

Mathew Hadfield

Isles Ferry

The MV Thomas Laighton, named for poet Celia Thaxter's dad, is the lifeline to the Isles of Shoals. It carries water, supplies and passengers. With no public dock at the Shoals, the ferry is the only way visitors can stop-over at the Isles, boarding at the Isles of Shoals Steamship Company in Portsmouth.

ABOVE

Marianne P. Young
Toward Newington

Modern industrial Portsmouth is much cleaner than in the 19th century when stacks polluted the air and factories infested the waters. Small towns like Newington have been sharply divided into industrial and shopping areas, leaving their historic hearts intact.

RIGHT

Sandy Agrafiotis
Salt Ship

Residents, in a local poll, revealed that the famous Portsmouth salt pile at Granite State Minerals is actually one of their favorite sites. Visiting cargo ships dwarf surrounding buildings, rising higher and higher in the river as they off load road salt, even as the chalky white pyramid grows.

The cooper or barrel maker was a well known artisan in colonial days. Visitors to Strawbery Banke may see a working Cooperage in the shade of an ancient tree. Preserving staples like wine, rum and ale were as important to early New Englanders as they are today.

TOP

Rockport Publishers
House Moving

Like many of the houses in Strawbery Banke, the Gov. Goodwin Mansion used to be elsewhere in town. During the 1960s and 70s preserved historic buildings rolled across town like portable Egyptian pyramids. Downtown residents might glance out a window and see an ancient wooden giant lumbering by.

Martha Brown
Horse Drawn

Horse-drawn carriages still clatter through downtown
Portsmouth, carrying passengers briskly though traffic. But
when they turn into Strawbery Banke, the cars and bustle and
years melt away. Passengers do not have to imagine life in
another era because they are literally there.

ABOVE

Marianne P. Young

In Tents Music

The Seacoast is permanent home to an astonishing number of artists who contribute to the region's high rating as a cultural destination point. During the summer and into the "shoulder" seasons, it is a rare night when live entertainers cannot be easily found.

LEFT

Marianne P. Young

Park Arts

In the late-1970s a grassroots cultural revival brought music and drama to what had been a decaying seaport area. Today the Prescott Park Arts Festival provides nonstop outdoor summer entertainment enjoyed by thousands daily.

BELOW LEFT

Marianne P. Young

Faire Play

Today Portsmouth's many annual festivals focus on chowder, blues, jazz, market square, road racing, children, chili, brewing, arts & crafts, sailing and more. The fall Renaissance Faire is the latest theme event in this culturally reborn city.

BELOW

Marianne P. Young

Mighty Gundalow

They were the pickup trucks of the Piscataqua. Scores of flat-bottomed boats called gundalows carried the bricks, farm animals and building supplies down the five-finger tributaries of the Piscataqua. Gone today, except for one reconstructed ship, the gundalows thrived when rivers were the early Seacoast highways.

OPPOSITE

Christopher Bishorek

A History of Revolution

One Fourth of July in the 1780s, John Paul Jones threw a party in Portsmouth that lit the night sky. Even before the battles at Lexington and Concord, this city had cast off its British leaders and New Hampshire had begun writing its own Constitution.

Marianne P. Young

Keeper's Light

A moody sky at the Whaleback keeper's house recalls this 1814 winter's tale. When a Spanish ship wrecked off Smuttynose at the rocky Isles of Shoals, survivors struggled toward the welcoming light of Sam Haley's solo cottage. Next day, legend, says, Haley found 14 frozen men, some nearly at his door.

ABOVE

Chris Fitt

Center of Attraction

Downtown Portsmouth has become a lightning rod for tourists visiting the region since the mid-1800s. In fact, 100 years earlier than that, Benjamin Franklin himself, legend says, installed one of the first metal lightning rods on the Warner House just two blocks up Daniel Street from the city center.

ABOVE

Jeremy Burnham
The Capt. Adams

In the 1980s the Piscataqua Gundalow Project reconstructed the "work horse" of the river that now sails the Seacoast. The Capt. Edward Adams was hauled to the river by oxen. Now the Ranger Foundation plans to rebuild an historic tall ship, originally built here and captained by John Paul Jones.

LEFT

Terry Chick
Great Endeavour

The Australian built replica of Captain Cook's famous ship Endeavour visited during the Seacoast's 375th settlement anniversary. As the tall ship made its way down the harbor among canon salutes, the captain remarked that Portsmouth gave the grandest welcome of all the ports he had visited in an east coast trek from Florida.

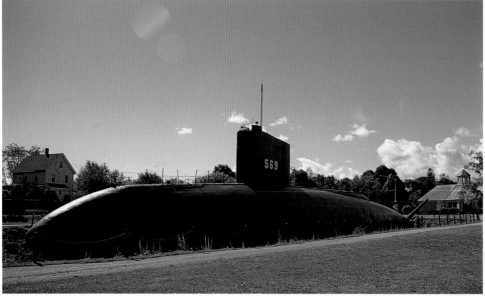

TOP

Edgar W. Ohman
Mall Muster

Seacoast residents barely blink on seeing their neighbors dressed in period costumes. Revived during the bicentennial, local militia members muster frequently for visitors. Whether here at Strawbery Banke, storming Fort William and Mary, camping on Exeter common or marching off to retake Quebec—these re-enactors keep history lively.

ABOVE

Rockport Publishers
USS Albacore

Once the fastest sub in the world, the USS Albacore travels the seven seas no more. A dedicated group of historians and engineers managed to float the Piscataqua-built sub to its final exhibition place where it is now open for tours to the public.

RIGHT

Stephen Gianotti
City Crossroads

Caught between the past and future, Portsmouth faces real concerns over how much more growth the city can handle. Once known for its timber and fish, the Port City adapted to shipbuilding and trading. Today it turns to tourism and clean high-tech industry—a tricky balancing act.

ABOVE

Mary Johanna Brown
River Mansion

Few cities in America offer more access to their past than the City of the Open Door. Today visitors can tour an ancient mansion like the Moffatt-Ladd House on Market Street. See the fascinating garden, unique architecture, famous Piscataqua furniture—all for less than a ticket to the movies.

ABOVE RIGHT

SPNEA
Christian Shore

Just across North Mill Pond beyond the ancient cemetery there is one of the oldest homes in New Hampshire. With a roof that stretches to the street, small triangular panes of leaded window glass and tiny rooms, the Jackson House feels like it belongs in the 1600s. Its doorway is a time capsule to another era.

RIGHT

SPNEA
Harbour Trail

With more than 70 downtown stops the historic Portsmouth Harbour Trail winds throughout the city. A more distant site, this is the back garden of the Rundlett-May House, open for tours on Middle Street. In 1807 it boasted all the modern home conveniences—including kitchen appliances, early central heating and a four-seater outhouse.

Ralph Morang
Mustard Muster

The mustard yellow John Paul Jones House, built in 1758, is one of the city's best known landmarks. Jones was born in Scotland, not here. It was Sarah Purcell's boarding house when the naval hero lodged here twice and today is home to the Portsmouth Historical Society.

Harry Lichtman
Twin Lights

Historians believe there has been a lighthouse on this New Castle
site since the 1600s. More functional, less scenic, the original colonial lighthouses were little more than a lantern on a tall pole.

NEW CASTLE

Bobby Conant
Wings Over Wentworth

An early "Hotel New Hampshire" owned by tycoon Frank Jones, Wentworth-by-the-Sea today is best known for its marina, golf course and seaside private homes. "The Ship" in the center was originally a theater, club and salt-water swimming area in the early 1900s.

Marianne P. Young
Piscataqua Café

Now a popular subject for touring photographers, the old Amazeen house in New Castle was once a waterfront café. Kittery, Maine is the shore visible in the background.

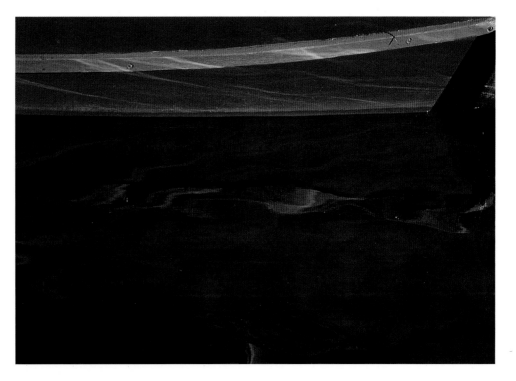

ABOVE

Marianne P. Young
Reflections

As small as it may be in land mass, the NH Seacoast seems to give back so much more to visitors and residents. As poets have long reminded us, there is something about the sea that mirrors the soul and washes troubles away.

LEFT

Harry Lichtman
Sailor's Delight

Not the Red Sea, but another Piscataqua sunset here along the bridge that leads to New Castle. Formerly "Great Island" the much sought-after colonial homes of New Castle once made up a rustic fishing village.

OPPOSITE
Harry Lichtman
Memory Lane

The smallest town in New
Hampshire, New Castle makes
up in longevity what it lacks in
geography. Today the winding
narrow streets still look like
they belong to an old European
fishing village.

ABOVE
Kimberly Lane
Faded Glory

Originally painted Nile green
in the late 1800s, Wentworth-
by-the-Sea became the ultimate
vacation resort for an exclusive
wealthy clientele. The battle to
preserve the surviving section
has waged in New Castle now
for two decades.

Marianne P. Young
Storm Clouds

After Indian Sagamore Passaconnaway died at the age of 100, a fierce period of Native American reprisals began. Traditional history focuses on a number of bloody colonial Indian "massacres" and not on the methodical extinction of the indigenous tribes that had occupied the Seacoast for thousands of years.

Harry Lichtman
Colonial Way

An ideal summer afternoon requires only a backpacked picnic lunch and a bicycle. Spend the entire afternoon exploring the serene byways that branch off the main New Castle road. Each new dead end path leads to another water view and classic colonial homes dating from the 1600s.

Judith A. Graham
Slip Away

The New Castle shoreline is dotted with docks, boat slips, small yacht clubs and marinas. On perfect summer days, it seems, half the population has abandoned the mainland, forgotten their cell phones, and slipped away to sea.

ABOVE

Marianne P. Young
Battle Creek

The "Back Creek" along the Kittery shore was once the start of a colonial plantation that stretched 30 miles up the Maine coast. Owner William Pepperrell was so determined to protect his fishing rights here that he marched 3,000 men to Nova Scotia to defeat the French at Louisburg in 1745.

RIGHT

Judith A. Graham
Prison Daze

Across the river from New Castle, the old Navy prison looks like a fantasy castle. This was Jack Nicholson's dreaded destination in the film "Last Detail". Finally, after decades of neglect, the imposing structure is being restored for commercial use.

ABOVE

Cathy Burns

Seacoast Sub Way

The arrival and departure of ships and submarines is an important part of the Piscataqua culture. Heavily fortified on both sites of the river, this area has never fired against an invading enemy. At the end of WW2 a number of German U-boats surrendered here and were escorted into Portsmouth Harbor.

OPPOSITE

Kimberly Lane

Swanny River

No, not Stratford-on-Avon, but Seacoast, New Hampshire. Swans are frequent visitors along the coast and especially in the Lamprey and Oyster Rivers. This regal figure was captured on film cruising the New Castle area.

NEXT PAGE, LEFT

Terry Chick

Twin Lights

New Hampshire actually has three ocean lighthouses. Whaleback, situated in the middle of the Piscataqua, and New Castle Light glow here. Further out to sea, isolated on White Island, is Granite State lighthouse number three. The day of the lighthouse keeper is gone—all three are now automated.

NEXT PAGE, RIGHT

Marianne P. Young

Come in Peace

Legend says that Native American leader Passaconnaway had a vision that white settlers would populate the land. His policy of peaceful relations greatly helped the colonists and led, sadly, to the displacement of his own people.

Judith A. Graham
Sanderson's Pond

On his famous visit to Portsmouth, George Washington reportedly stopped in Greenland en route. Stepping from his carriage, he mounted his white horse and road the final miles at the head of a majestic parade that still lives in local memory.

GREENLAND, RYE
& NEWINGTON

ABOVE

Marianne P. Young
They Came to Fish

This region was, above all else, a fisherman's heaven. Captain John Smith of Pocahontas fame visited in 1614 and wrote that the fish near Monhegan Island in Maine and around the Isles of Shoals were so plentiful that one could scarcely drop anchor without hitting one.

OPPOSITE

Katherine M. Hodgeman
Regal Seagull

Basking in its own glory, the Jenness Beach seagull is the most visible, but by no means the most plentiful winged resident of the Seacoast. Visitors who tour the nearby Great Bay Estuary are given a checklist of over 250 local bird species that may be spotted in this area.

Jeremy Burnham

Lobster Laws

They may look pretty hanging on this shed in Rye, but tourists beware of floating lobster pot markers. Lobstermen will tell you they have the right to shoot poachers on sight, and colorful local legends tell of turf wars between fishermen and naive cityfolk.

RIGHT

Kevin & Sue Psaros

Parade of Sail

Like paper hats upon a gentle pond, but don't be fooled. Poet John Greenleaf Whittier warned how a sunny day off the coast of Rye could turn tragic when sudden storms appear.

BELOW

Terry Chick

Coming Together

The popular Children's Museum with the Seacoast Science Center in Rye are among the region's best known "kid centers" with nonstop hands-on activities. At the turn of last century this site was the hub of activity for local African-Americans for whom this church was a family and spiritual centerpiece.

Eric H. O'Brien
Leaves Alone

Those who live among New England seasons, as
disparate as compass points, wonder how others
live elsewhere. The dramatic "leaf peeper" season
has drawn tourist since the mid-19th century.
Ironically, train and trolley passengers were able to
make this scenic pilgrimage easier, cheaper and
sometimes faster than they can in the 21st century.

Maggie Burns
Ancient Roots

We can only imagine the great trees that once
dominated the region. Not far from this spot in
Rye, at Odiorne's Point, the ocean sometimes
remembers. When the tide is very low, the stumps
of a petrified forest stretch seaward toward the
Isles of Shoals.

ABOVE

Rockport Publishers

Rye Harbor

If you blink and miss the road by Saunders Lobster, you miss
Rye Harbor, accessible by a dead end road amid a piled granite
breakwater dotted with wild rosehips. Don't blink if you can help it.

OPPOSITE

Mathew Hadfield

Sandy Beach

Beaches like this one at Rye (formerly "Sandy Beach") are precious
sights on the brief New Hampshire coast. Portsmouth has no beach
of its own, but is situated between the white sandy NH beaches and
those of South Coast Maine just to the north.

Heather L. Pickering

Timeless Sea

What length people will go to just to reach the ocean. This, we can be certain, is what the first European settlers saw when they arrived in New Hampshire in 1523. This, we can say too, is what our lost Native American predecessors saw for 10,000, perhaps twice that many years before.

Sara J. Pluta

Perfect Storm

Only the hardiest of winter rental tenants need dig out from underneath the latest nor'easter. Here at Wallis Sands in Rye, half the population is elsewhere, in places where the sun does shine and the wind doesn't rattle windows with a sudden gale.

Marianne P. Young

Comin' Thru to Rye

With much of the region's precious marshland already filled or inhabited, the wild remaining area becomes even more precious. This marshy area in Rye, due to controlled growth, appears much as it has for centuries.

Scott Hakala

East to West

Early land grants to New Hampshire included land all the way to New York fanning out like a giant triangle from this tiny bit of coast. In a burst of growth, colonial governor Benning Wentworth granted land for 200 new towns including Bennington, Vermont when that state was also part of NH.

ABOVE

Marianne P. Young
Straws Point

Day or night, in any weather, two short coastal drives never fail to kick start a dull soul into full gear. Take the loop around New Castle or this oceanfront stretch in Rye. Open the windows and smell the air. Get some steamers. Life is going to be okay.

OPPOSITE

Marianne P. Young
Viking Rock

Rocks at Rye appear at first glance like breaching whales so common in these cold Atlantic waters. Some believe our first European visitors were actually Vikings who followed the migrating whales and arrived here in time to celebrate the first millennium.

OPPOSITE

Marianne P. Young
Lunar Shipment

Large ships and tankers must navigate the Piscataqua when the tide allows. In the 1970s, tycoon Aristotle Onassis promised the region prosperity if he was allowed to offload oil into a pipeline here off the coast of Rye. In an exercise of NH town democracy, a few hundred citizens voted to reject the multi-million dollar deal.

ABOVE

Jane Pedersen
Ice Cycles

In all recorded history you could count the times the mighty Piscataqua has frozen on the frigid fingers of one hand. But down her icy tributaries, it's another story. This Rye scene, on the other hand, feels on the verge of thaw when the maples run free and the sugar sap boils.

ABOVE

Harry Lichtman

Bay View

For Native Americans, this was the inland
highway. Great Bay and Little Bay connect the Seacoast by routes long forgotten. From here a dugout canoe could reach the falls at what
became the mills of Dover, Newmarket, Durham and Exeter.

LEFT

Harry Lichtman

Great Bay

The "inner ocean" of the salt water Great Bay has a shoreline twice the length
of the entire New Hampshire Atlantic coast. Still largely unspoiled, the tidal
bay is a natural haven for birds, small mammals, fish and abundant shellfish.

OPPOSITE

Trish Simas

Greenland Harvest

Often overlooked by Seacoast travelers, Greenland is among the lovely towns
off the beaten path. A hop off Route 101, Greenland has its own coastline
along the inner Great Bay, first explored by Martin Pring in 1603. Like other
old farming towns—Newfields, Newington, Stratham—Greenland center is
worth seeking out.

ABOVE

John J. Veneski

In Training

The nearby University of New Hampshire championship hockey team lends inspiration to young skaters. On a winter afternoon these junior athletes are a familiar site on the frozen rivers and ponds of the Piscataqua region.

LEFT

Douglas Bulko

Berrys Brook

The waterways of Seacoast NH are a complex array of tidal pools, salt and fresh water rivers, marshes, bays, coves, inlets, rock and beach. Once called "Sandy Beach", the town of Rye not only governs a substantial slice of oceanfront and four Isles of Shoals, but inland spots like here at tranquil Berry's Brook.

RIGHT

Maggie Burns

Smoke Screen

Hollywood "effects" wizards go to great expense to re-create the evocative atmospheres that Nature provides Seacoast visitors for free, as here in Rye Harbor. Films about this region have, ironically, been shot elsewhere—in Nova Scotia, Toronto, Virginia and elsewhere.

Sara J. Pluta

The Coast Road

Bikers speed past rubbernecking drivers as they navigate the scenic serpentine route 1A that hugs the shoreline of Rye. Riding by summer mansions with their stunning rocky views, we all whisper to ourselves "If only, if only."

Maggie Burns

Future Habitat

Allowing the land room to breathe, scientists know, is essential to coastal life. The close proximity of the University of New Hampshire promotes environmental study. Surprising statistics show that the region is today more densely forested than it was in the early 1700s when colonial clear-cutting denuded the land.

Gregory E. Smart
Goody's Soul

Poor Goodwife Cole, New Hampshire's only woman convicted of
witchery in the wake of the Salem hysteria. Jailed and spurned, the
elderly woman was later pardoned. But here in Hampton, they say,
when the sky is right, you can see her spirit streaking off to heaven.

EABROOK & THE HAMPTONS

Kevin & Sue Psaros

Berry Berry Good

Pick-Your-Own farms remain a Seacoast tradition, featuring an amazing array of apples, vegetables and berries, even Christmas trees. This ripe raspberry farm is a popular Hampton Falls spot.

OPPOSITE

Trish Simas

War and Peace

Although no historic battles have been fought in the Seacoast, New Hampshire contributed heavily to the nation's armed conflicts. NH soldiers outnumbered all other states in the Battle of Bunker Hill, for example. Also black NH soldiers, though many were enslaved, fought in the Revolution and Civil War.

ABOVE

Katherine M. Hodgeman

Returning Monarch

How convenient for the Seacoast that it lies in the migration path of the Monarch Butterfly. How convenient for the butterfly that the famous Fuller Gardens in North Hampton is on its winged itinerary.

ABOVE

Jeff Winterton
Morning

As the Hampton sun rose Colonial Gen. Jonathan Moulton awoke to find his new young bride quivering in their bed. What had frightened her so? During the night, she cried, the General's first wife, recently dead, had reached up from under the bed and stolen back her old wedding ring.

LEFT

Judy Silverwood
Tug of War

If you were a child here you'd remember the hot coins in your hand while you searched for the perfect kite at Herb Philbrick's famous store. The wrapping off, the string held taut, the kite rose as your brother ran alongside. Tethered, until the rude dusk breeze stole your prize, that kite tugged back like the pull of life itself.

BELOW

Jeff Winterton
Wet Suit Optional

Although just 18 miles long, the smallest coastline in America, the NH shore attracts a dedicated group of surfers. Yes, the water is very cold, but off the rocky Hampton shore, it's still possible to hang ten chilly digits.

James S. Barrington
Surf n' Turf

At times the seacoast landscape seems to realign itself suddenly in layers. Here the bold promontory at Boar's Head has been sandwiched between the waves and clouds of an oncoming storm.

Linda Tyler
Perfect Plaice

One imagines that Tintoretto or Michelangelo, with all his painterly skill, would have found Plaice Cove the fitting backdrop for some vast Italian chapel ceiling. This Hampton sunrise still has the power to stir the soul as a postcard in a gift shop mall.

Paul Watson
Mist Opportunity

Those who truly love the sea, embrace it in every mood. Local lore is rich with tales of mariners so skilled that they could navigate the treacherous rocky shores merely by the sound of waves against familiar ledges. Tourists, meanwhile, tend to leave the hazy seasons behind.

John Wichroski

Fishin' to Fusion

New England absorbs change, yet remains mysteriously the same. Today the region is called the e-Coast for its high proportion of technology companies. Here fishing boats in Seabrook remind us of the original reason Europeans came to this frigid region. That ancient industry co-exists today with the Seabrook Station nuclear power plant.

IN SILENCE REST

James S. Barrington
In Silence Rest

The sea is a cemetery for countless lost mariners.
Stories of shipwreck and drowning abound—from
the lost Spanish sailors on Smuttynose Island to
the submarines Squalus and Thresher. This
Hampton Beach statue reminds us to take pause.

ABOVE RIGHT

Rockport Publishers
People Who Love People

Generations of families have come, year after year,
to the white sands of Hampton and "the strip"
featuring live bands, fireworks and the century-old
Hampton Casino. Poet John Greenleaf Whittier
used to pitch a lone tent here and enjoy a solitude
now exchanged for action.

RIGHT

Mathew Hadfield
Hampton State

Summer graduates leave Hampton State Park
tanned and trim and ready to face the workplace
with a smile. Some 250,000 of them may be "on
campus" at the state park on any hot July day.
A gigantic salt-water swimming facility is
conveniently located nearby.

BELOW RIGHT

Mathew Hadfield
North Hampton

Originally part of Hampton, this region was
largely farm country and retained a small steady
population until its recent growth spurt. Today a
variety of small public and private beach spots
offer an alternative to the densely popular strip
at Hampton Beach.

LEFT

Andrew C. Ryan
Town Hall

The "town meeting" concept so trendy among
politics today is a centuries old tradition in New
Hampshire. In two dozen Seacoast town halls, as
here in Hampton Falls, and across the state, locals
gather to make their opinions known.

BELOW LEFT

Joan L. Ganotis
Equine Eden

Kentucky Derby winner Dancer's Image was
among the famous horses raised in wilds of North
Hampton. Not far from the open ocean, the
morning mist rolls though a local farm.

OPPOSITE

Kevin & Sue Psaros
Hidden Chapel

Here and there, amid the quiet woods, a hiker
comes upon a tiny chapel that it seems, for the
moment, no one else has ever found. This is Union
Chapel in North Hampton.

Paul Watson

Hampton Falls

Originally one of the first New Hampshire settlements, Hampton is now divided into Hampton Falls, South Hampton, North Hampton and Hampton Beach. Collectively they form a NH version of "The Hamptons."

ABOVE

Linda Tyler
Golden Shore

The sun seems especially fond of Hampton's North Beach and often presents the shoreline there with an exceptionally rich dawn. Rocks, joggers, dogs and their masters all stand like dark paper cutouts against the glow. In what seems like moments, the Midas touch dissolves into morning.

TOP

Paul Watson
Good Night, Sweet Day

Victorian visitors to the Seacoast would stand on the porch of their hotel at sunset. As the day disappeared below the horizon, a rich solo voice would sing an emotional farewell—Good night, sweet day.

Jeff Winterton

Unearthly Palette

Long before computer graphics, Seacoast visitors witnessed hues of red that seem to come from another world. Surprise bursts of violet, orange, pink, lavender and salmon may suddenly announce the end of a far less colorful day.

ABOVE

Marianne P. Young

Fragile Beauty

With the growth of the Seacoast economy comes responsibility to maintain the tenuous balance between humans and nature. Delicate ecosystems, many believe, have reached their maximum capacity—and none is more precious than the wetlands. Concerned locals maintain a vigilant eye on population growth, watershed management and endangered wildlife.

Jane Pedersen
Moonlight Murder

Among the region's most haunting legends is that of Louis Wagenr who
rowed 10 miles on a moonlit March night to the tiny island of
Smuttynose in 1873. This Hampton moon recalls the bloody night retold
in a bestseller and film called "The Weight of Water."

INDEX OF PHOTOGRAPHERS

Jeff Winterton
Pondering

Throughout this book we find photographers, not visible perhaps, but omnipresent. They wait in quiet places, measuring rays of light, tilting to the left or right to shape the little camera frame. Then in a snap, the moment frozen, they move off, leaving us to ponder where they've been.